The Back Country

Gary Snyder

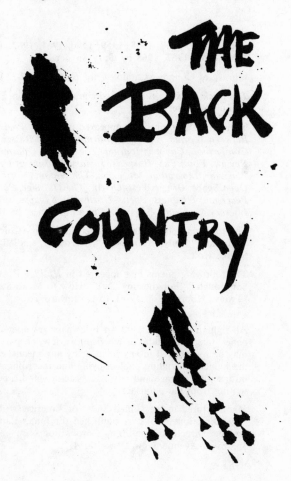

THE
BACK
COUNTRY

A New Directions Book

Library of Congress Catalog Card Number: 67-23491

The Back Country is published simultaneously in England by Fulcrum Press.

Some of these poems first appeared in: *Beloit Poetry Journal, Between Worlds, Big Table, Burning Water, Bussei, Cleft, Combustion, Coyote's Journal, The Critical Quarterly, Evergreen Review, Foot, Fux, Harper's, Joglars, Journal of Creative Behavior, Liberation, Magazine, The Nation, Northwest Review, Open Space, Orient West, Origin, The Outsider, Paris Review, Peace and Gladness, Poetry Northwest, Synapse, Writing, The Yale Literary Magazine, Yũgen,* and in a broadsheet by Bob Ross.

The following poems first appeared in *Poetry* (Chicago): "February," "July," "August," "November," and "Through the Smoke Hole."

The following poems first appeared in *Holiday*: "August on Sourdough," "For the Boy . . .," "How to Make Stew," "Twelve Hours . . .," "Work to Do toward Town," and "7:IV:64."

Manufactured in the United States of America.
New Directions Books are published for James Laughlin by New Directions Publishing Corporation,
333 Sixth Avenue, New York 10014

Contents

III   KALI

V   MIYAZAWA KENJI

For Kenneth Rexroth

GAR WEST

A BERRY FEAST

For Joyce and Homer Matson

1

Fur the color of mud, the smooth loper
Crapulous old man, a drifter,
Praises! of Coyote the Nasty, the fat
Puppy that abused himself, the ugly gambler,
Bringer of goodies.

> In bearshit find it in August,
> Neat pile on the fragrant trail, in late
> August, perhaps by a Larch tree
> Bear has been eating the berries.
> > high meadow, late summer, snow gone
> Blackbear
> > eating berries, married
> To a woman whose breasts bleed
> From nursing the half-human cubs.

> > Somewhere of course there are people
> > collecting and junking, gibbering all day,

"Where I shoot my arrows
"There is the sunflower's shade
> — song of the rattlesnake
> coiled in the boulder's groin
"K'ak, k'ak, k'ak!
> sang Coyote. Mating with
> humankind —

> The Chainsaw falls for boards of pine,
> Suburban bedrooms, block on block
> Will waver with this grain and knot,
> The maddening shapes will start and fade
> Each morning when commuters wake —
> Joined boards hung on frames,
> > a box to catch the biped in.

> > and shadow swings around the tree
> Shifting on the berrybush
> > from leaf to leaf across each day
> The shadow swings around the tree.

13

2

Three, down, through windows
Dawn leaping cats, all barred brown, grey
Whiskers aflame
          bits of mouse on the tongue

Washing the coffeepot in the river
          the baby yelling for breakfast,
Her breasts, black-nippled, blue-veined, heavy,
Hung through the loose shirt
          squeezed, with the free hand
                    white jet in three cups.
Cats at dawn
          derry derry down

Creeks wash clean where trout hide
We chew the black plug
Sleep on needles through long afternoons
          "you shall be owl
          "you shall be sparrow
          "you will grow thick and green, people
          "will eat you, you berries!
Coyote: shot from the car, two ears,
A tail, bring bounty.

     Clanks of tread
               oxen of Shang
               moving the measured road

Bronze bells at the throat
Bronze balls on the horns, the bright Oxen
Chanting through sunlight and dust
          wheeling logs down hills
          into heaps,
                    the yellow
     Fat-snout Caterpillar, tread toppling forward
     Leaf on leaf, roots in gold volcanic dirt.

When
Snow melts back
          from the trees
Bare branches   knobbed pine twigs
          hot sun on wet flowers
Green shoots of huckleberry
Breaking through snow.

Belly stretched taut in a bulge
Breasts swelling as you guzzle beer, who wants
              Nirvana?
Here is water, wine, beer
Enough books for a week
A mess of afterbirth,
A smell of hot earth, a warm mist
Steams from the crotch

"You can't be killers all your life
"The people are coming —
        — and when Magpie
Revived him, limp rag of fur in the river
Drowned and drifting, fish-food in the shallows,
"Fuck you!" sang Coyote
        and ran.

Delicate blue-black, sweeter from meadows
Small and tart in the valleys, with light blue dust
Huckleberries scatter through pine woods
Crowd along gullies, climb dusty cliffs,
Spread through the air by birds;
Find them in droppings of bear.

   "Stopped in the night
   "Ate hot pancakes in a bright room
   "Drank coffee, read the paper
   "In a strange town, drove on,
        singing, as the drunkard swerved the car
   "Wake from your dreams, bright ladies!
   "Tighten your legs, squeeze demons from
        the crotch with rigid thighs
   "Young red-eyed men will come
   "With limp erections, snuffling cries
   "To dry your stiffening bodies in the sun!

   Woke at the beach. Grey dawn,
   Drenched with rain. One naked man
   Frying his horsemeat on a stone.

4

Coyote yaps, a knife!
Sunrise on yellow rocks.
People gone, death no disaster,
Clear sun in the scrubbed sky
                    empty and bright
Lizards scurry from darkness
We lizards sun on yellow rocks.

    See, from the foothills
    Shred of river glinting, trailing,
    To flatlands, the city:
        glare of haze in the valley horizon
    Sun caught on glass gleams and goes.
    From cool springs under cedar
    On his haunches, white grin,
        long tongue panting, he watches:

Dead city in dry summer,
Where berries grow.

MARIN-AN

sun breaks over the eucalyptus
grove below the wet pasture,
water's about hot,
I sit in the open window
& roll a smoke.

distant dogs bark, a pair of
cawing crows; the twang
of a pygmy nuthatch high in a pine —
from behind the cypress windrow
the mare moves up, grazing.

a soft continuous roar
comes out of the far valley
of the six-lane highway — thousands
and thousands of cars
driving men to work.

SIXTH-MONTH SONG IN THE FOOTHILLS

In the cold shed sharpening saws.
      a swallow's nest hangs by the door
setting rakers in sunlight
falling from meadow through doorframe
      swallows flit under the eaves.

Grinding the falling axe
sharp for the summer
      a swallow shooting out over.
over the river, snow on low hills
sharpening wedges for splitting.

Beyond the low hills, white mountains
and now snow is melting.   sharpening tools;
      pack horses grazing new grass
bright axes — and swallows
      fly in to my shed.

THE SPRING

Beating asphalt into highway potholes
   pickup truck we'd loaded
road repair stock shed & yard
a day so hot the asphalt went in soft.
   pipe and steel plate tamper
took turns at by hand
then drive the truck rear wheel
a few times back and forth across the fill —
finish it off with bitchmo round the edge.

the foreman said let's get a drink
& drove through woods and flower fields
   shovels clattering in back
into a black grove by a cliff
   a rocked in pool
   feeding a fern ravine
      tin can to drink
numbing the hand and cramping in the gut
surging through the fingers from below
   & dark here —
let's get back to the truck
get back on the job.

A WALK

Sunday the only day we don't work:
Mules farting around the meadow,
                    Murphy fishing,
The tent flaps in the warm
Early sun: I've eaten breakfast and I'll
                 take a walk
To Benson Lake. Packed a lunch,
Goodbye. Hopping on creekbed boulders
Up the rock throat three miles
             Piute Creek —
In steep gorge glacier-slick rattlesnake country
Jump, land by a pool, trout skitter,
The clear sky. Deer tracks.
Bad place by a falls, boulders big as houses,
Lunch tied to belt,
I stemmed up a crack and almost fell
But rolled out safe on a ledge
             and ambled on.
Quail chicks freeze underfoot, color of stone
Then run cheep! away, hen quail fussing.
Craggy west end of Benson Lake — after edging
Past dark creek pools on a long white slope —
Lookt down in the ice-black lake
             lined with cliff
From far above: deep shimmering trout.
A lone duck in a gunsightpass
             steep side hill
Through slide-aspen and talus, to the east end,
Down to grass, wading a wide smooth stream
Into camp. At last.
        By the rusty three-year-
Ago left-behind cookstove
Of the old trail crew,
Stoppt and swam and ate my lunch.

TRAIL CREW CAMP AT BEAR VALLEY, 9000 FEET. NORTHERN SIERRA — WHITE BONE AND THREADS OF SNOWMELT WATER

Cut branches back for a day —
trail a thin line through willow
   up buckbrush meadows,
   creekbed for twenty yards
 winding in boulders
   zigzags the hill
into timber, white pine.

gooseberry bush on the turns.
hooves clang on the riprap
   dust, brush, branches.
   a stone
 cairn at the pass —
strippt mountains hundreds of miles.

sundown went back
   the clean switchbacks to camp.
bell on the gelding,
stew in the cook tent,
black coffee in a big tin can.

FIRE IN THE HOLE

Squatting a day in the sun,
      one hand turning the steeldrill,
one, swinging the four pound singlejack hammer
                         down.
three inches an hour
granite bullhump boulder
              square in the trail.
above, the cliffs,
              of Piute Mountain waver.
sweat trickles down my back.

why does this day keep coming into mind.
a job in the rock hills
      aching arms
             the muletracks
                  arching blinding sky,
     noon sleep under
             snake-scale juniper limbs.

that the mind
      entered the tip of steel.
the arm fell
      like breath.
the valley, reeling,
             on the pivot of that drill —
twelve inches deep we packed the charge
      dynamite on mules
            like frankincense.
Fire in the hole!
Fire in the hole!
Fire in the hole!

jammed the plunger down.
thru dust
            and sprinkling stone
strolld back to see:
hands and arms and shoulders
free.

BURNING THE SMALL DEAD

Burning the small dead
      branches
broke from beneath
  thick spreading
          whitebark pine.

        a hundred summers
snowmelt   rock   and air

hiss in a twisted bough.

  sierra granite;
        mt. Ritter —
        black rock twice as old.

Deneb, Altair

windy fire

HOME FROM THE SIERRA

Woke once in the night, pissed,
checkt the coming winter's stars
built up the fire
still glowing in the chilly dawn.

Washing the mush pot in the lake
frost on the horse turds
a grayjay cased the camp.

All morning walking to the car
load up on granite stone,
seedling sugar pine.

Down to hot plains.
Mexicans on flatcars in the San Joaquin.
cool fog
smell of straw mats
cup of green tea
by the Bay.

FOXTAIL PINE

bark smells like pineapple: Jeffries
cones prick your hand: Ponderosa

nobody knows what they are, saying
"needles three to a bunch."

  turpentine tin can hangers
  high lead riggers

"the true fir cone stands straight,
the doug fir cone hangs down."

— wild pigs eat acorns in those hills
cascara cutters
tanbark oak bark gatherers
myrtlewood burl bowl-makers
little cedar dolls,
  baby girl born from the split crotch
   of a plum
  daughter of the moon —

foxtail pine with a
clipped curve-back cluster of tight
 five-needle bunches
 the rough red bark scale
and jigsaw pieces sloughed off
  scattered on the ground.
— what am I doing saying "foxtail pine"?

these conifers whose home was ice
age tundra, taiga, they of the
  naked sperm
do whitebark pine and white pine seem the same?

 a sort of tree
 its leaves are needles
 like a fox's brush
(I call him fox because he looks that way)
 and call this other thing, a
  foxtail pine.

A HEIFER CLAMBERS UP

a heifer clambers up
    nighthawk goes out
        horses
trail back to the barn.
    spider gleams in his
        new web
dew on the shingles, on the car,
    on the mailbox —
the mole, the onion, and the beetle
    cease their wars.
        worlds tip
into the sunshine, men and women
    get up, babies crying
children grab their lunches
    and leave for school.
the radio announces
    in the milking barn
        in the car bound for work
"tonight all the countries
    will get drunk and have a party"
russia, america, china,
        singing with their poets,
pregnant and gracious,
    sending flowers and dancing bears
        to all the capitals
fat
    with the baby happy land

AUGUST ON SOURDOUGH,
A VISIT FROM DICK BREWER

You hitched a thousand miles
                    north from San Francisco
Hiked up the mountainside   a mile in the air
The little cabin — one room —
                    walled in glass
Meadows and snowfields,   hundreds of peaks.
We lay in our sleeping bags
                    talking half the night;
Wind in the guy-cables   summer mountain rain.
Next morning I went with you
                    as far as the cliffs,
Loaned you my poncho —   the rain across the shale —
You down the snowfield
                    flapping in the wind
Waving a last goodbye   half hidden in the clouds
To go on hitching
                    clear to New York;
Me back to my mountain   and far, far, west.

OIL

soft rainsqualls on the swells
south of the Bonins, late at night. Light
from the empty mess-hall
throws back bulky shadows
of winch and fairlead
over the slanting fantail where I stand.

but for men on watch in the engine room,
the man at the wheel, the lookout in the bow,
the crew sleeps. in cots on deck
or narrow iron bunks down drumming
passageways below.

the ship burns with a furnace heart
steam veins and copper nerves
quivers and slightly twists and always goes —
easy roll of the hull and deep
vibration of the turbine underfoot.

bearing what all these
crazed, hooked nations need:
steel plates and
long injections of pure oil.

THE WIPERS SECRET

Down in the bilges
or up out of sight on the bulkheads
time after time
year after year
we paint right over the dirt.

The first engineer
he knows.
but what can he say?
the company says
save time.

ONCE ONLY

almost at the equator
almost at the equinox
  exactly at midnight
    from a ship
     the full

     moon

in the center of the sky.

Sappa Creek near Singapore
March 1958

AFTER WORK

The shack and a few trees
float in the blowing fog

I pull out your blouse,
warm my cold hands
    on your breasts.
you laugh and shudder
peeling garlic by the
    hot iron stove.
bring in the axe, the rake,
the wood

we'll lean on the wall
against each other
stew simmering on the fire
as it grows dark
     drinking wine.

27

ROLLING IN AT TWILIGHT

Rolling in at twilight — Newport Oregon —
    cool of september ocean air, I
saw Phil Whalen with a load of groceries
    walking through a dirt lot full
    of logging trucks, cats
      and skidders

    looking at the ground.

I yelld as the bus wheeld by
    but he kept looking down.
    ten minutes later with my books and pack
      knockt at his door

" Thought you might be on that bus "
      he said, and
    showed me all the food.

HITCH HAIKU

They didn't hire him
       so he ate his lunch alone :
the noon whistle

     •   •   •

Cats shut down
       deer thread through
men all eating lunch

     •   •   •

Frying hotcakes in a dripping shelter
                Fu Manchu
Queets Indian Reservation in the rain

                •   •   •

A truck went by
                three hours ago:
Smoke Creek desert

                •   •   •

Jackrabbit eyes all night
        breakfast in Elko.

                •   •   •

Old kanji hid by dirt
on skidroad Jap town walls
                down the hill
to the Wobbly hall

                                        Seattle

                •   •   •

Spray drips from the cargo-booms
a fresh-chipped winch
                spotted with red lead
young fir —
                soaking in summer rain

                •   •   •

Over the Mindanao Deep

Scrap brass
                dumpt off the fantail
falling six miles

                •   •   •

[*The following two were written on classical
themes while travelling through Sappho, Washington.
The first is by Thomas L. Hoodlatch.*]

Moonlight on the burned-out temple —
          wooden horse shit.

Sunday dinner in Ithaca —
          the twang of a bowstring

     ●   ●   ●

After weeks of watching the roof leak
          I fixed it tonight
by moving a single board

     ●   ●   ●

*A freezing morning in October in the high
Sierra crossing Five Lakes Basin to the
Kaweahs with Bob Greensfelder and Claude Dalenburg*

Stray white mare
          neck rope dangling
forty miles from farms.

       ●   ●   ●

Back from the Kaweahs

Sundown, Timber Gap
         — sat down —
             dark firs.
   dirty;   cold;
too tired to talk

      ●   ●   ●

Cherry blossoms at Hood river
                    rusty sand near Tucson
mudflats of Willapa Bay

    ●   ●   ●

Pronghorn country

Steering into the sun
                    glittering jewel-road
shattered obsidian

    ●   ●   ●

The mountain walks over the water!
Rain down from the mountain!
                    high bleat of a
cow elk
            over blackberries

    ●   ●   ●

A great freight truck
                lit like a town
through the dark stony desert

    ●   ●   ●

Drinking hot saké
                        toasting fish on coals
        the motorcycle
out   parked in the rain.

    ●   ●   ●

Switchback

turn, turn,
and again,   hard-
scrabble
steep travel a-
head.

HOW TO MAKE STEW IN THE PINACATE DESERT
RECIPE FOR LOCKE & DRUM

A. J. Bayless market bent wire roller basket buy up parsnips, onion,
carrot, rutabaga and potato, bell green pepper,
& nine cuts of dark beef shank.
They run there on their legs, that makes meat tasty.

Seven at night in Tucson, get some bisquick for the dumplings.
Have some bacon. Go to Hadley's in the kitchen right beside the
frying steak — Diana on the phone — get a little plastic bag from
Drum —
Fill it up with tarragon and chili; four bay leaves; black pepper
corns and basil; powdered oregano, something free, maybe about
two teaspoon worth of salt.

Now down in Sonora, Pinacate country, build a fire of Ocotillo,
broken twigs and bits of ironwood, in an open ring of lava: rake
some coals aside (and if you're smart) to windward,
keep the other half ablaze for heat and light.
Set Drum's fourteen-inch dutch oven with three legs across the
embers.

Now put in the strips of bacon.
In another pan have all the vegetables cleaned up and peeled and
sliced.
Cut the beef shank meat up small and set the bone aside.
Throw in the beef shank meat,
And stir it while it fries hot,
lots of ash and sizzle — singe your brow —

Like Locke says almost burn it — then add water from the jeep
can —
add the little bag of herbs — cook it all five minutes more — and
then throw in the pan of all the rest.
Cover it up with big hot lid all heavy, sit and wait, or drink bud-
weiser beer.

And also mix the dumpling mix aside, some water in some
bisquick,
finally drop that off the spoon into the stew.
And let it cook ten minutes more
and lift the black pot off the fire
to set aside another good ten minutes,
Dish it up and eat it with a spoon, sitting on a poncho in the dark.

13.XII.1964

FAR

EAST

YASE: SEPTEMBER

Old Mrs. Kawabata
cuts down the tall spike weeds —
                    more in two hours
than I can get done in a day.

out of a mountain
of grass and thistle
she saved five dusty stalks
                    of ragged wild blue flower
and put them in my kitchen
                    in a jar.

PINE RIVER

for Tetsu

From the top of
        Matsue castle
miles of flat ricefields
hills, and a long lake.
a schoolboy looks through a
home made telescope
        over the town.

new stores dwarf
this hilltop tower,
diving dolphins on the
        roof like horns —
nobody now quite
knows how they hoisted
        huge cut stone.

the Matsudaira family
owned it all,
sat in this windy
        lookout spire
in winter: all their
little villages
under snow.

VAPOR TRAILS

Twin streaks twice higher than cumulus,
Precise plane icetracks in the vertical blue
Cloud-flaked light-shot shadow-arcing
Field of all future war, edging off to space.

Young expert U.S. pilots waiting
The day of criss-cross rockets
And white blossoming smoke of bomb,
The air world torn and staggered for these
Specks of brushy land and ant-hill towns —

    I stumble on the cobble rockpath,
Passing through temples,
Watching for two-leaf pine
    — spotting that design.

in Daitoku-ji

MT. HIEI

I thought I would
sit with the screens back
and sing: watching the
half gone   moon rise late
but my hands were too numb
to play the guitar
the song was cold mist
the wine wouldn't warm
so I sat at the border
of dark house and moon
in thick coat — seeing stars rise
back of the ridge.
like once when a lookout
I took Aldebaran
for fire.

OUT WEST

In the cross field
all day a new gas cultivator
cough cough   down each row
frizzing the soil, fine chopper "friable"

before it was cucumber,
    the boy in a straw hat
    clumsily turns at the end of a run
                    shifting levers,

through deodar limbs come the gas fumes
    cucumber vines
    poles and straw ropes
    torn down, two crops a summer,

last year the family
was out there with hoes.
the old woman dead now?

one-eyed chop tongue rotary
bucks and wheezes,

    that straw hat shaped like a stetson
        wearing those tight blue jeans.

Kyoto

AMI   24.XII.62

Hair a wild stroke of black
            on white
                    pillow —
knees flexing up playing
            white sheets and gown,
gold-brown grass on the hillside
            clouds over twisted pine
            jabs of rain down from Mt. Hiei
"we never thought he'd be a boy"

nobody home at the house
            the father has gone off to teach
            the light at the gate is still on
"he's been printing on broken stone"
                    thru the window.

lettuce and onions no matter how cold.
does he know? that he has a new boy?

the dog has stoppt barking
sits shivering
and shivering
            tied to the woodshed door frame.

THE PUBLIC BATH

the bath-girl

>   getting dressed, in the mirror,
>   the bath-girl with a pretty mole and a
>   red skirt is watching me:
>   am I
>   different?

the baby boy

>   on his back, dashed with scalding water
>   silent, moving eyes
>   inscrutably
>   pees.

the daughters

>   gripping and scrubbing his two little daughters
>   they squirm, shriek at
>   soap-in-the-eye,
>   wring out their own hair
>   with grave wifely hands,
>   peek at me, point, while he
>   soaps up and washes their
>   plump little tight-lip pussies
>   peers in their ears,
>   & dunks them in hot tile tub.
>   with a brown-burnt farmboy
>   a shrivelled old man
>   and a student who sings *silent night.*

>   — we waver and float like seaweed
>   pink flesh in the steamy light.

the old woman

>   too fat and too old to care
>   she just stands there
>   idly knocking dewy water off her
>   bush.

the young woman

        gazing vacant, drying her neck
        faint fuzz of hair
        little points of breasts
           — next year she'll be dressing
               out of sight.

the men

        squatting soapy and limber
        smooth dense skin, long muscles —

        I see dead men naked
        tumbled on beaches,
               newsreels, the
                 war

A VOLCANO IN KYUSHU

Mount Aso   uplands
horses, rimrock

        the sightseeing buses crammed.
        to view bare rock, brown grass,
               space,
        sulphury cliffs, streakt snow.
    — whiffing the fumaroles
a noseless, shiny,
mouth-twisted middle aged man.

bluejeans, check shirt, silver buckle,
J. Robert Oppenheimer:
        twenty years ago
        watching the bulldozers
          tearing down pines
            at Los Alamos.

ASLEEP ON THE TRAIN

Briefcase, tight garter
        over the knees
        peep of fat little thighs
roll and lean with the fall of the train

        eyes
shut. mouth open. so young women
tire with the rest   tired workers.
jerk with the speedup and slow

go-ahead signals flash by
the Special Express
has only one stop

where they wake from their trance
to themselves.

EIGHT SANDBARS ON THE TAKANO RIVER

Well water
cool in
summer

warm in
winter

white radish root
a foot long
by its dark
dirt hole
green top
her son.

cherry blossoms

the farmer never looks up
the woman serves sake
the tourists are sick or asleep

gone wild
straw berry vine
each year more small
sour
mulcht by pine.

white peeld logs
toppld in sap
scalpt branch
            spring
                    woods

dragonfly
why wet moss
        your black
        stretch-stretch-
wing perch

strawberrytime

walking the tight-rope
high over the streets
with a hoe and two buckets
                    of manure.

straight-
swaying stride
            backt
twelve-foot
        pine pole
            lightly,
on her head.

FOUR POEMS FOR ROBIN

Siwashing it out once in Siuslaw Forest

I slept under   rhododendron
All night   blossoms fell
Shivering on   a sheet of cardboard
Feet stuck   in my pack
Hands deep   in my pockets
Barely able   to sleep.
I remembered   when we were in school
Sleeping together   in a big warm bed
We were   the youngest lovers
When we broke up   we were still nineteen.
Now our   friends are married
You teach   school back east
I dont mind   living this way
Green hills   the long blue beach
But sometimes   sleeping in the open
I think back   when I had you.

A spring night in Shokoku-ji

Eight years ago this May
We walked under cherry blossoms
At night in an orchard in Oregon.
All that I wanted then
Is forgotten now, but you.
Here in the night
In a garden of the old capital
I feel the trembling ghost of Yugao
I remember your cool body
Naked under a summer cotton dress.

An autumn morning in Shokoku-ji

Last night watching the Pleiades,
Breath smoking in the moonlight,
Bitter memory like vomit
Choked my throat.
I unrolled a sleeping bag
On mats on the porch
Under thick autumn stars.
In dream you appeared
(Three times in nine years)
Wild, cold, and accusing.
I woke shamed and angry:
The pointless wars of the heart.
Almost dawn. Venus and Jupiter.
The first time I have
Ever seen them close.

December at Yase

You said, that October,
In the tall dry grass by the orchard
When you chose to be free,
"Again someday, maybe ten years."

After college I saw you
One time. You were strange.
And I was obsessed with a plan.

Now ten years and more have
Gone by: I've always known
      where you were —
I might have gone to you
Hoping to win your love back.
You still are single.

I didn't.
I thought I must make it alone. I
Have done that.

Only in dream, like this dawn,
Does the grave, awed intensity
Of our young love
Return to my mind, to my flesh.

We had what the others
All crave and seek for;
We left it behind at nineteen.

I feel ancient, as though I had
Lived many lives.

And may never now know
If I am a fool
Or have done what my
      karma demands.

THE LEVELS

wild cat kittens
born in the ceiling
       play sky gods
thundering over the room.
       was it claude in the night?
was it thieves?

       above our northbound steps
the wild cat brood walks west

a hawk sails over the roof
a snake went under the floor

       how can hawks hunt in the rain?

I walk through the hallway:
the soul of a great-bellied cloud.

THE FIRING

for Les Blakebrough and the memory of John Chappell

Bitter blue fingers
Winter nineteen sixty-three A.D.
       showa thirty-eight
Over a low pine-covered splay of hills in Shiga
West-south-west of the outlet of Lake Biwa
Domura village set on sandy fans of the sweep
       and turn of a river
Draining the rotten-granite hills up Shigaraki
On a nineteen-fifty-seven Honda cycle model C
Rode with some Yamanashi wine "St Neige"
Into the farmyard and the bellowing kiln.
Les & John
In ragged shirts and pants, dried slip
Stuck to with pineneedle, pitch,
       dust, hair, woodchips;

Sending the final slivers of yellowy pine
Through peephole white blast glow
No saggars tilting yet and segers bending
             neatly in a row —
Even their beards caked up with mud & soot
Firing for fourteen hours. How does she go.
Porcelain & stoneware: cheese dish. twenty cups.
Tokuri. vases. black chawan
Crosslegged rest on the dirt eye cockt to smoke —

The hands you layed on clay
Kickwheeld, curling,
             creamd to the lip of nothing,
And coaxt to a white dancing heat that day
Will linger centuries in these towns and loams
And speak to men or beasts
When Japanese and English
Are dead tongues.

WORK TO DO TOWARD TOWN

Venus glows in the east,
             mars hangs in the twins.
Frost on the logs and bare ground
             free of house or tree.
Kites come down from the mountains
And glide quavering over the rooftops;
             frost melts in the sun.
A low haze hangs on the houses
      — firewood smoke and mist —
Slanting far to the Kamo river
             and the distant Uji hills.
Farmwomen lead down carts
             loaded with long white radish;
I pack my bike with books —
             all roads descend toward town.

NANSEN

I found you on a rainy morning
After a typhoon
In a bamboo grove at Daitoku-ji.
Tiny wet rag with a
Huge voice, you crawled under the fence
To my hand. Left to die.
I carried you home in my raincoat.
" Nansen, cheese! " you'd shout an answer
And come running.
But you never got big,
Bandy-legged bright little dwarf —
Sometimes not eating, often coughing
Mewing bitterly at inner twinge.

Now, thin and older, you won't eat
But milk and cheese. Sitting on a pole
In the sun. Hardy with resigned
Discontent.
You just weren't made right. I saved you,
And your three-year life has been full
Of mild, steady pain.

SIX YEARS

January

      the pine tree is perfect

Walking in the snowhills the trail goes just right
Eat snow off pine needles
     the city's not so big, the
         hills surround it.
Hieizan wrapped in his own cloud —
Back there no big houses, only a little farm shack
       crows cawing back and forth
        over the valley of grass-bamboo
           and small pine.

If I had a peaceful heart it would look like this.
      the train down in the city

    was once a snowy hill

February

water taps running, the sun part out
cleaning house   sweeping floor
knocking cobwebs off the shoji   pap pap
wiping the wood and the mats with a wet rag
hands and knees on the veranda
cat-prints — make them a footwiper
             of newspaper
wash the motorcycle.   fold clothes
start a new fire under the kama.
fill Mrs. Hosaka's kerosene stove tank,
get the cat hairs
out of the kotatsu.
take the sheets in from the bamboo poles
     where they're drying
put away the poles
stand them up below the eaves and
tie them with strings.
scrub out the floor of the bath and move the
         mirror

and towel rack
sweep out the genkan footprints
oil the clutch cable of the motorcycle
through the oil nipple under the handle grip
— take off sweater now because it's
too hot
put back on the denim jacket   work
Nansen mews angrily because he feels so sick
all the different animals are persons

what will I do about *Liberation*.
6:30   bath
charcoal.   black.   the fire part red
the ash pure white

March

Up in dirt alley
eat korean food
drink white doboroku out of bowls
broil strips of beef & liver over coals
finish off with raw cow's womb
in sauce, jade-white and oyster smooth
piss against the slab posts of the highways
overhead,
bar girl girl-friend with a silver trinket cup
hung on a neck-chain, she, gives us,
all beer free.

sift through night streets,
Kato, Nagasawa, me, Sakaki,
okinawan awamori bar
clear glasses full up to the brim
like flavord gin — must millet —
with choppt onion.
whirl taxi by
glass door opening sharks, their,
eyeballs to the sky —
in coffee, tight butt tress;
to station where the world trains meet
I south around the loop
yellow writhing dragon full of drunks
& hall the windy concrete of
Zojoji.

April

Firework bangs echo up the valley
    a twelve-foot snake banner
    glides off a bamboo pole at the top of a pine
two hundred people for lunch.
black umbrellas drying in the sun
— wash the red lacquer bowls
    and arrange on trays;
        cherry
    white blooms through the hilly country.

in the back right, lotus root
agé, konyaku, and a mikan.
front center sliced vinegared
    cucumber and udo.
middle, sweet red beans and
    salt yellow pickles.
front right soup
    white floating tofu
front left a tall red bowl with a bowl-like
lid full of white steaming rice;
back left, low bowl with a round cake
    of special-fried tofu under the lid.

used trays come back
wash in heated water:
a wood tub three feet wide
drain in a five-foot basket
    on bamboo grating,
dry lacquer-ware twice and stow it in boxes
    carry them up to the
    right front corner of the white-plastered
store house
        joined to the temple by a plank
        over the mud out back where
        corrugated iron sheets tilt
            over stacks of short firewood.

zokin in buckets of water.
wipe the long wood beams
wipe the feet of the Buddha
wipe under bronze incense stands

firecrackers boom from the shrine down the road
    five *go* of vinegar, four *go* of sugar
    five *sho* of rice;

old women half double scuttle to toilets
hoisting kimono   enroute to the door

the PA loudspeaker plays songs, plays the chants
        of the priests in the hall, the
            Dai-Hannya, Perfection
                of Wisdom

at Dragon Cloud Temple.
Five Hundred year Festival over
        they load in the busses
        or walk to their farms.

we wash ricepots, teacups, and bowls
baskets, dippers, buckets, and cauldrons,
take a bath, drink saké, and eat.
sitting on stools in the high-ceilingd kitchen

wind in the fir and the pine —
get under the quilts laid out on the mats
talk in the dark, and sleep.

May

    Sitting and resting on the crest, looking far
out over Yokkawa
to a corner of Ohara —
Sugi and fir and maple on the half-logged hill

    A delicate little hawk floats up
hunting delicate little country mice to eat.   Lute
Lake; the noble Sugi — a tree as great as Redwood, Douglas
Fir, Sequoia, Red Cedar, Sugar Pine.

    (To hell with all these cultures — history
after the Jurassic is a bore.   Sugi like Sequoia;
Hinoki like a cedar)

    Light wind, warm May sun & old woman bundling
brush by the trail —
men planing beams in a cool tin-roof shed
for the new Shaka-dō — fine double-edged saws
hand worn brush-hooks
battered jikatabi, funny breeches, cotton head-things
like the Navajo —
relit cigarette butts, sturdy walkers — hills and trails
of rocks and trees and people.

    Quiet grey-wood copper-roofed old temple.   Down
and off into the Ogi village fields, and on along
steep ridges through bamboo brush to Ohara, Jakko-in.
Jizo there with his bug-scare clanker staff

    (Night ride America; thin-lipped waitress whores —)

        students listen to the tapes —
Miss Nunome in a green dress
    she usually wears something open at the neck a dab.
Yamada-kun who can't look or answer straight
    yet seems not stupid
            " A nap is ' provisional sleep ' "

Blue jumper on a white blouse (Miss Yokota)
                            car honks outside
Pink fur sunset
Miss   ?   in a crisp white pleated skirt falling in
            precise planes — her cheeks ruddy with rouge
            " people call her ' Janie ' "
            " people collar Janie "

Van Gogh print on the wall: vase of flowers all yellow
                & tawny.
Sun setting on Atago Mountain

    " strength   strap   strand   strut   struck
      strum   strung   strop   street   streak "

    " cord   ford   gorge   dwarf   forth   north
      course   horse   doors   stores   dorm   form
      warp   sort   short   sport   porch "

    pingpong game in the hall
Motorcycle rumbles in the streets —
horns — dark nights rain up sudden on the tin bar
            roof next door

    " try tea   buy ties   weigh Tim   buy type
      flat tea   bright ties   greet Tim   met Tess
      stout trap   wet trip   right track   light tread
      high tree   Joy tries   gay trim   fry tripe "

Why that's old Keith Lampe's voice, deep & clear

    " ripples   battles   saddles   doubled   dazzled
      wondered   hammered   eastern   western   southern "

Language torn up like a sewer or highway
& layed out on text
Page and tape.

July

kicking through sasa
      bear grass bamboo
         pass into thickets.
     dowse a wand knocking down spider
       net us on all sides
       sticky and strong

chirrr; semi
  hangs under   bamboo leaf

      in the heat
     sweat
  kick through sasa
snaking uphill in thickets

below, taro
  terraces down to the beach.
swim among mild red jellyfish

     a woman pickt shells, stoopt over
          bare breasted
     kneedeep in seaweed rocks
     her two boys
      play in the tall cliff
        shade

cross away.
     from bamboo to pinegrove
     three axes
        someone
     naps under a tree

August

night   town of lights
at sea
    unpainted rough prowed squid fishers
boats with their gas mantle lamps
miles off shore.
                counted two hundred.
                wind curls on the salt-
                   sticky chest, caked ribs
      sticky sea

day dodging sun
    zigzagging barefoot
    on blistering rocks
    to dive, skim under reefs
          down along ledges
    looking for oysters or snails
          or at fish

night without blanket
sleeping on sand.
        the
    squid-fisher lights.
one-lung two-cycle engines

they sleep all day under the eaves
              headland houses
    half-naked on mats.
    the wives gather shells
    coarse-tongued, sun black
    or working at carrying rocks
    for the new coast road

      eating big lunch balls
      of cold rice.

tobacco and grapes on the dunes.
some farmers come down to the beach
in the dark   white lanterns
    sending out rowboats, swinging
a thousand-foot net
    five times down the length of the beach.
we help haul
            tumbling pockets

               glittering eyes and white bellies —
          a full-thighed young woman
          her dress tucked up in her pants
                    tugs and curses
        an old man calling
          across the dark water sculling

the last haul a yard-wide ray
        she snaps off his switching
               devil-tail stinger
          & gives us three fish.

they beach their boats
full of nets
their lamps bob over the dunes

we sleep in the sand
and our salt.

September

     Rucksack braced on a board, lashed tight on back,
sleeping bags, map case, tied on the gas tank
sunglasses, tennis shoes, your long tan in shorts
north on the west side of Lake Biwa
Fukui highway still being built,
          crankcase bangd on rocks —
               pusht to the very edge by a blinded truck
    I saw the sea below beside my knee:
you hung on and never knew how close.

     In Fukui found a ryokan cheap
washt off each other's dust by the square wood tub
ate dinner   on worn mats
          clean starcht yukata
          warm whisky with warm water,
all the shoji open, second floor,
          told each other
     what we'd never said before, ah,
          dallying on mats
               whispering sweat
          cools our kissing skin —

next morning rode the sunny hills, Eihei-ji,
got the luggage rack arc-welded
back through town and to the shore,
    miles-long spits and dunes of pine

and made love on the sand

October

The Rich have money; Give to the Rich!
  —J.C.: " All suffering is self-willed."
    you CAN take it with you
    [THE OTHERWORLD FORWARDING SERVICE
    leave your money with us;
    we'll get it through] —
Low-order Tantric phenomena.

    " God in cinders; wreck on child."

J.C.'s law — " You can't get out of the same trap
until you get into it."   Hemp
    " retted " with dew or water; then the fibers
    " scutched "
Somehow life has been like . . . every day is Flag Day for me . . .
Cold turkey   with all the tremens

    [File your absence
    with NULL & VOID
       — Gilt-edged Insecurities —
    loose ends bought in vacant lots
        & the
    NOWHERE VACUUM TRUST]

      says the Armpit from Outer Space.

" 1000 shares of *mikan* futures " (she's a
    Kshatriya — hell yes,
    let her run things)

Promiscuity: they sell themselves short.
          All
        Dragon-Riders

All,   Dharma Kings.

November

hoeing the hataké, pull out all the clover bulb —
long white root stem, deep
    and other long roots.
" those daikon will rot in December, the frost;
    smoothing the row.
" this daikon will live through the winter.
but it don't taste so good as the other

white lime sprinkld on fresh turnd furrows like snow
these acid soils.   see that daikon?
    all yellow because the ground sourd.
tiny gobo seeds, grow into twisty two foot long roots.

        spinach seeds next
soaked over night in warm water
left from the bath.   makes them germinate quick.

dump weeds from the wheelbarrow back in the bamboo grove
peas planted in double rows, making holes
             four inches apart
with fore finger, stick in two seeds
          poke it in
    later fertilize all with the dippers
    yoke of wood buckets, that " human " smell
    not near so bad as you think

clean off these heavy heavy boots
when the soil is all tilld and the winter seeds
sowed
        casts of mud
        with the back of a sickle
        stooping in gravel

December

Three a.m. — a far bell
    coming closer:
fling up useless futon on the shelf;
outside, ice-water in the hand & wash the face.
    Ko the bird-head, silent, skinny,
    swiftly cruise the room with
    salt plum tea.

Bell from the hondo chanting sutras.   Gi:
deep bell, small bell, wooden drum.
    sanzen at four
    kneel on icy polisht boards in line;

Shukuza rice and pickles
barrel and bucket
dim watt bulb.
    till daybreak nap upright.
                sweep
    garden and hall.
    frost outside
            wind through walls

At eight the lecture bell.   high chair.
Ke helps the robe — red, gold,
    black lacquer in the shadow
    sun and cold

Saiza a quarter to ten
soup and rice dab on the bench
feed the hungry ghosts
    back in the hall by noon.
two o clock sanzen
three o clock bellywarmer
    boild up soup-rice mush.
dinging and scuffing.   out back smoke,
             and talk.

At dusk, at five,
black robes draw into the hall.
    stiff joints, sore knees bend
    the jiki pads by with his incense lit,
                bells,

wood block crack
& stick slips round the room
on soft straw sandals.

seven, sanzen
tea, and a leaf-shaped candy.
kinhin at eight with folded hands —
      single-file racing in flying robes leaning
                  to wake —

nine o clock one more sanzen
ten, hot noodles,
three bowls each.

Sit until midnight.   chant.
      make three bows and pull the futon down.
      roll in the bed —
      black.

A far bell coming closer

Envoy to Six Years

Down in the engine room again
Touching a silver steam line
         with a tiny brush.
Soogy the oil sump — gloves and rags —
— " how long you say you been Japan?
      six years eh you must like the place.
      those guys in New York
                  bunch of fuckin crooks.
      they ain't just selling
      little two-bit caps, they making books."

Rinse out the soogy rag in kerosene,
And wipe off sooty oil condenser line
Driving forward geared turbine —
The driveshaft treetrunk thick,
Bearings bathed in flowing oil,

The belly of the ship.

On a corpse / dread / laughing /
four arms / a sword / a severed head /
removing fear / giving/
wearing skulls / black / naked

III

When I went down
to sea-lion town
my wife was dead
the canoes were gone

ALYSOUN

My mother called you Robin.
I curst your blisters
when we fought brush
hunting the trail
in the forest gorge of the Elwha —
forded creeks and found the path,
climbed three switchback miles
to camp and cook   by dark.
You whimpered all night long
with evil dreams
in a tossing bed by me
under the low limbs of a Silver fir.

TO HELL WITH YOUR FERTILITY CULT

To hell with your Fertility Cult, I
never did want to be fertile,
you think this world is just
a goddamn oversize cunt, don't you? Everything
crowding in and out of it like a railway
terminal   and isn't that nice?
all those people going on trips.
well this is what it feels like, she said,
— and knocked the hen off the nest, grabbed
an egg and threw it at him, right in the face,
the half-formed chick half clung, half slid
half-alive, down over his cheekbone, around
the corner of his mouth, part of it thick
yellow and faintly visible bones and it drippt
down his cheek and chin
— he had nothing to say.

FOR A STONE GIRL AT SANCHI

half asleep on the cold grass
          night rain flicking the maples
under a black bowl upside-down
on a flat land
          on a wobbling speck
smaller than stars,
                    space,
the size of a seed,
          hollow as bird skulls.
light flies across it
          — never is seen.

a big rock weatherd funny,
old tree trunks turnd stone,
          split rocks and find clams.
                    all that time
loving;
two flesh persons changing,
          clung to, doorframes
          notions, spear-hafts
in a rubble of years.
                    touching,
this dream pops. it was real:
          and it lasted forever.

ROBIN

I always miss you —
last fall, back from the the mountains
you'd left San Francisco
now I'm going north again
                as you go south.

I sit by a fire at the ocean.
How many times I've
hitchhiked away;
                the same pack on my back.

Rain patters on the rhododendron
cloud sweeps in from the sea over sand dunes
and stoopt lodgepole pine.

Thinking of the years since we parted.
last week I dreamed of you —
buying a bag of groceries
                for Hatch.

Sutton Lake, Oregon, 16 June 1954

NORTH BEACH ALBA

waking half-drunk in a strange pad
making it out to the cool gray
        san francisco dawn —
white gulls over white houses,
        fog down the bay,
tamalpais a fresh green hill in the new sun,
driving across the bridge in a beat old car
        to work.

COULD SHE SEE THE WHOLE REAL WORLD
WITH HER GHOST BREAST EYES SHUT
UNDER A BLOUSE LID?

" A woman smells like fresh-plowed ground "
" A man smells like chewing on a maple twig "
Rockslides in the creek bed;
       picking ferns in the dark gorge.

Goldwire soft short-haired girl, one bare leg up.
Cursing the morning.
      " it's *me* there's no — "

Yellow corn woman on the way to dead-land
      by day a dead jackrabbit,
      by night a woman nursing her live baby.
Bridge of sunflower stalks.
Nursing a live baby.
                daytime, dead-land, only a hill.
Cursing the morning.
" My grandmother said they stepped single
& the hoof was split " — deer

Yellow corn girl
Blue corn girl
Squawberry flower girl

" Once a bear gets hooked on garbage there's no cure."

NIGHT

All the dark hours everywhere repairs
and rights the hearts & tongues of men
and makes the cheerful dawn —

the safe place in a blanket burrow
hissing in ears and nibbling wet lips
smoothing eyebrows and a stroke up the back of the knee,
licking the nape of the neck and tickling the tense
breast with fluttering eyelid, flitting
light fingers on thin chest skin,
feeling the arteries tangle the hollow groin,
arching the back backward, swinging sidewise,
      bending forward, dangling on all fours.

the bit tongue and trembling ankle,
joined palms and twined legs,
the tilted chin and beat cry,
hunched shoulders and a throb in the belly.
teeth swim in loose tongues, with toes curled.
eyes snapped shut, and quick breath.
hair all tangled together.

the radio that was never turned off.
the record soundlessly spinning.
the half-closed door swinging on its hinges.
the cigarette that burned out.
the melon seeds spit on the floor.
the mixed fluids drying on the body.
the light left on in the other room.
the blankets all thrown on the floor and the birds
      cheeping in the east.
the mouth full of grapes and the bodies like loose leaves.
the quieted hearts, passive caress, a quick exchange
      of glances with eyes then closed again,
the first sunlight hitting the shades.

A DRY DAY JUST BEFORE THE RAINY SEASON

DRUNK last night
    drunk the night before

talking and shouting and laughing, maybe
I should've been home reading —
" all right *don't* leave me alone —
    do something with me then ! "
          the landlady's son
heard through a back wall window.

Sunday morning, november, plenty of birds
a pair of red-shafted flickers
       on the peach tree
    stretch wings
      showing the white-flash back
      linnets crack seeds at the feed tray.

Not too hung over —
I suppose I'll get drunk tonight.
one year : from rain to wistaria,
apricot blossoms, all night singing,
     sleeping on the floor,
off to work in the Sierra
     back in august
    cool fog, dryness,
leaves on the fruit trees fall.

Soon the rain starts again.
smell of burning leaves.
orange berries, red berries a
     sudden jump cat
       —I know him —
bee rattles in a flower
    this warm sober day

I wonder what I said to everybody

ANOTHER FOR THE SAME

a cut reed floating
a sort of Lady Komachi
wiser than me
the best of your beauty

always hidden, yū 和歌
" a glow of red leaves in dark woods "
in your gray eyes.
look at me stranger
I've been hungry, alone, cold,
but not lonely
must I be lonely with you?
Danae to sunlight, starlight,
wind, snuffing it on every
       high hill
of the mind.

you really are going nowhere
I wish I was going with you.
to rock, to space
   — I cannot shake this love of mine
which is so much less
than yours.

THIS TOKYO

Peace, war, religion,
Revolution, will not help.
This horror seeds in the agile
Thumb and greedy little brain
That learned to catch bananas
With a stick.
      The millions of us worthless
To each other or the world
Or selves, the sufferers of the real
Or of the mind — this world
Is but a dream? Or human life
A nightmare grafted on solidity
Of planet — mental, mental,
Shudder of the sun — praise
Evil submind freedom with de Sade
Or highest Dantean radiance of the God
Or endless Light or Life or Love
Or simple tinsel angel in the
Candy heaven of the poor —
Mental divinity or beauty, all,
Plato, Aquinas, Buddha,
Dionysius of the Cross, all
Pains or pleasures hells or
What in sense or flesh
Logic, eye, music, or
Concoction of all faculties
& thought tend — tend — to this:
      This gaudy apartment of the rich.
The comfort of the U.S. for its own.
The shivering pair of girls
Who dyked each other for a show
A thousand yen before us men
— In an icy room — to buy their relatives
A meal. This scramble spawn of
Wire dirt rails tin boards blocks
Babies, students, crookt old men.
      We live
On the meeting of sun and earth.
We live — we live — and all our lives
Have led to this, this city,
Which is soon the world, this
Hopelessness where love of man

Or hate of man could matter
None, love if you will or
Contemplate or write or teach
But know in your human marrow you
Who read, that all you tread
Is earthquake rot and matter mental
Trembling, freedom is a void,
Peace war religion revolution
Will not help.

27 December 1956

KYOTO FOOTNOTE

She said she lived in Shanghai as a child
And moved to Kobe, then Kyoto, in the war;
While putting on her one thin white brassiere.
She walked me to the stair and all the girls
Gravely and politely said take care,
    out of the whorehouse into cool night air.

THE MANICHAEANS

for Joanne

Our portion of fire
        at this end of the milky way
(the Tun-huang fragments say, Eternal Light)
Two million years from M 31
        the galaxy in Andromeda —
My eyes sting with these relics.
Fingers mark time.
        semen is everywhere
Two million seeds in a spurt.

Bringing hand close to your belly
        a shade off touching,
Until it feels the radiating warmth.

Your far off laughter
Is an earthquake in your thigh.
Coild like Ourabouros
        we are the Naga King
This bed is Eternal Chaos
                — and wake in a stream of light.

Cable-car cables
Whip over their greast rollers
Two feet underground.
        hemmed in by mysteries
        all moving in order.
A moment at this wide intersection,
Stoplights change, they are
        catastrophes among stars,
A red whorl of minotaurs
                        gone out.
The trumpet of doom
        from a steamship at Pier 41.

Your room is cold,
        in the shade-drawn dusk inside
Light the oven, leave it open
Semi transparent jet flames rise
                        fire,
Together we make eight pounds of
Pure white mineral ash.

Your body is fossil
As you rest with your chin back
    — your arms are still flippers
                your lidded eyes lift from a swamp
Let us touch — for if two lie together
Then they have warmth.

We shall sink in this heat
                of our arms
Blankets like rock-strata fold
                dreaming as
                Shiva and Shakti
And keep back the cold.

ARTEMIS

Artemis,
Artemis,
so I saw you naked —
well GO and get your goddam'd
        virginity back

me, me,
I've got to feed my hounds.

MADLY WHIRLING DOWNHILL

madly whirling downhill
      THE WITCH
who can make the electric lights go out
who can, as she sits in her apartment under the street
                  make you follow.

the two of them lived for years
in an old house in town.
no one ever came to see about bills
no one ever entered or left it
            that house.

he knows what the end will be
calm and he doesn't care,
         there is no one, no way
            to save him.

XRIST

Your hanging face I know, I know your tree.
You can't hide under Hebrew
            & I don't pity you
Burning yourself alive in Athens to impress the mob
Having your last wild fling — in drag — at the altar —
            robed in cornstarch
            and stolen Toltec jewels
                  Ziggurat rotgut
Cutting your own balls off — dog priests — kybele
The mincing step — shy glance — Graves thot you lame
Horrified virgin dropping in a pool.

whipping the bullshit roarer
Your flayed penis flaring
Gold wrought infibula
      — circumcized girls.

New World popcorn, Polynesian spit —
Dropping a log on the couple where they fuck
        the dance, the whips,
Saviour of Man!
    — who put the hell to be harrowed?

The bruisd snake coils in the grass
He is wise;
       there are trees in high places;
Keep your blood off the crotch of our tree.

MORE BETTER

Uncle,   Oh uncle
  seventy dogs

O centipede
     bit me in bed
wind in the red leaf berry tree

     whynes

Bull you are
too brown.

The Persimmon
was too fat   the tree its

branches too bent down.

FOR PLANTS

The ancient virgin
picking mushrooms
in the damp forest
gloom

      Peyotl
        dream-child bud
glowing in hollow desert
     HO   hands
    gather the holy baby
faceted jewel bush
              child of the
sky is solid rainbow
           squash maiden
           corn girl

hair prongs   seedbed root
suck magic from dirt, rains
   wash down rainbow
and bury him under the floor.

long trumpet of thornapple flower
datura highsmoke
scoopt in blanket
   james. town. weed.

gum of hashish
passt through the porthole
bumboat to tanker

   half-glimpst
  " glow of red lips in dark hair "
   slave-of-god-dancer

hidden
      in glittering fall.

ear, eye, belly
      cascara   calamus

cut bark is vapor
of paradise odor —
brick for a pillow

rolld in a blanket,
                    to see

Artemis naked:
the soft white
                buried sprout
of the world's first
seed.

WHAT DO THEY SAY

The glimpse of a once-loved face
                gone into a train.
Lost in a new town, no one knows the name.
        lone man sitting in the park
Chanced on by a friend
                of thirty years before,
                what do they say.
Play chess with bottle caps.
        " for sale " sign standing in the field:
                dearest, dearest,
Soot on the sill,
        a garden full of weeds

THE SIX HELLS OF THE ENGINE ROOM

The Hot Air Hell of the fiddley where rails
are too hot to touch and your shoes burn

The oily cramp Hell of the bilges
painting underside pipes — saltwater and oil
ankledeep slosh in the shoe.

Inside-the-boiler Hell, you go in through a
hot brick hole where it's black
and radiates heat

Back of the boilers-Hell soogying valve-wheels
                              and flanges

Shaft Alley Hell getting rubbed by the rough
spinning shaft

Paint Locker Hell, it smells fumes,
your hands get all sticky.

MAYA

                    for Peter Orlovsky

white clothes — white skin —
white cows —
          the dream of India —
                and flowers —
teeth stained red,
hair silver
like that old Jain jeweller
wouldn't touch meat

a little *O* now and then

MOTHER OF THE BUDDHAS, QUEEN OF HEAVEN, MOTHER OF THE SUN; MARICI, GODDESS OF THE DAWN

for Bhikku Ghosananda

old sow in the mud
bristles caked black
down her powerful neck

tiny hooves churn
squat body slithering
deep in food dirt

her warm filth,
deep-plowing snout,
dragging teats

those who keep her
or eat her
are cast out

she turns her small eye
from earth to
look up at me.

Nalanda, Bihar

WANDERING THE OLD, DIRTY COUNTRIES

— in your clean overalls
   who's poor?
             Evtushenko or the
             shop foreman won't say.
I'm not speaking for America,
But for poets —
             well yes malnutrition
Bad teeth, shit-stained babies
Flies around the eyes,
And nobody pities them
             but the humanist bourgeoisie
             and the Komsomol kids.

             over the jolting buses
Bustards   loosefeathered
Vultures hunched on hills

That fat baby flesh, *kohl* eyes
             feed them well.
Them soviets, them
U.S. men
Helping.

ON OUR WAY TO KHAJURAHO

On our way to
        Khajuraho
the bus stoppt, we ate
        guavas
cheap.
             a toilet
with a picture of a woman and a man,
                      two doors,
             in the square
dusty village somewhere on the way.

            a girl thirteen
                  gave pice in change
to an old woman bought some sweets;
the men of Bundelkhand
wear elf-tongued
            flowery leather shoes.

she must have been low caste.
the girl stood off
                  little coins
crosst from hand to hand

ANURADHAPURA CITY OF THE PLEIADES

for Joanne

Anuradhapura city of the Pleiades
                  is
            cool and grassy
underfoot.
white monkeys, white
            granite
      posts lie tumbled crisscross
            white
dome stupa with the spire tower gold

network oak like
her black dress on
kneeling thighs
      making a rubbing
                  on the foot floor
      moon shape stone;
lion, elephant, geese;
ring below the stairs.

of all the buildings nothing but a plinth.
      us married;
meadows of new grass.

CIRCUMAMBULATING ARUNACHALA

for centuries sadhus live and die
in dolmen rock-slab huts near
      Arunachala

Small girls with gaudy flowers
flash down the bare walk road,
      the weight, the power,
the full warm brilliance of the human mind
      behind their eyes:
          they die or sicken in a year.

Below the hill —
wells, ponds, spiky trees,
carvd fragments of soft bodies,
      female bellies,
          centuries old.

I can't look out over cities without thinking of carpenters,
plumbers, hod-carriers, cement-mixer truck drivers, plasterers

how many hours were they paid for to build up Seattle, or Port-
land, (which has such dark carpets — such white fir skulls —)
skeleton lathe behind plaster laid on so cool — creamy under the
trowel — dries to a powder, spidery lines. block bricks, shake roofs

san francisco white stairstep-up rooflines. stucco & tile houses
laid out in rows in the Sunset — photos after the quake the weird
frames of half-broken buildings. lunchpails in unfinished walls —
how long since eyes laid on that rafter

in the hills they cast mud & fire it for rooftiles — the gray waves
of Kyoto — highschool kids study their english or math in cramp
ceilinged second floor rooms to the racket of looms on the ground
floor, the shimmering heat of the sun-facing southward scree
roof —

new buildings reinforced concrete strung full of wiring and
piping, Plant in the basement — walls knock in the night — laundry
ghosts chatter on flat modern roofs looking off at the shrine forest
hills

the drainage of streets, hollow mountains in rows, noisy with
alien molecules burning at speeds past belief, how they sift — how
they clutter —

layers of mohenjo-daro, nine cities deep, a kiln at the end of the
age built out in the street

forests are covered with mud and asbestos, the riverbeds sucked
up and cast into plates hung on melted-down oxides

mankind your bowels are as grinding and heavy as those which
forced leaves into coal, burned sand to obsidian; you draw up and
lead along water, your arm rises and falls, you break through things
as they are.

NANAO KNOWS

for Nanao Sakaki

Mountains, cities, all so
        light, so loose.   blankets
Buckets — throw away —
Work left to do.
        it doesn't last.

Each girl is real
        her nipples harden, each has damp,
        her smell, her hair —
— What am I to be saying.
There they all go
Over the edge, dissolving.

Rivetters bind up
Steel rod bundles
For wet concrete.
In and out of forests, cities, families
        like a fish.

LYING IN BED ON A LATE MORNING

Lying in bed on a late morning
A new girl beside me,
        I hardly know —

Half-awake, dreaming,
I smile the smile,
        you smile, when you sing.

Dreaming and smiling,
   dream of your long smooth legs.

LOOKING AT PICTURES TO BE PUT AWAY

Who was this girl
In her white night gown
Clutching a pair of jeans

On a foggy redwood deck.
She looks up at me tender,
Calm, surprised,

What will we remember
Bodies thick with food and lovers
After twenty years.

THE TRUTH LIKE THE BELLY
OF A WOMAN TURNING

for Ali Akbar Khan

The truth
like the belly of a woman turning,
       always passes by.
       is always true.

throat and tongue —
    do we all feel the same?
      sticky hair curls

quivering throat
pitch of jaw
       strung pull
    skinnd turn, what will
  be the wrack
       of all the old —

who
cares.
    CRYING
all these passt,
      losst,
        years.

' It always changes "
wind child
wound child

MOTHERS AND DAUGHTERS
live oak and madrone.

FOR JOHN CHAPPELL

Over the Arafura sea, the China sea,
   Coral sea, Pacific
chains of volcanoes in the dark —
you in Sydney where it's summer;
I imagine that last ride outward
late at night.
               stiff new gears — tight new engine
up some highway I have never seen
too fast — too fast —
    like I said at Tango
        when you went down twice on gravel —

Did you have a chance to think
o shit I've fucked it now
instant crash and flight and sudden death —

    Malaya, Indonesia
    Taiwan, the Philippines, Okinawa
        families sleeping — reaching —
        humans by the millions
        world of breathing flesh.

me in Kyoto.   You in Australia
wasted in the night.
black beard, mad laugh, and sadly serious brow.
    earth lover;   shaper and maker.
        potter, cooker,

    now be clay in the ground.

1964

HOW MANY TIMES

We walk down streets together
          switching hip globes
          clean skin, neat smell,

why these clothes.
breast, the bra,   stitch & buckle — soft —

(sweaty farm girl on the road to
Yasé   sold me bunch of daikon
nipples brushing bare along
the blue work-jacket seam —)

above the bottom part the hose is browner
         held by funny things.
         bulge of thigh — softest skin of all —

now   am I all right? ah.
presst down,   open,
    were I   as open,

    we shall do this
        how
    many times.

TASTING THE SNOW

The family — the little family —
    table edge and napkin wipe
    the warm   you hold in your arms
    children, saliva, washt clothes
Hand-holds and curves of the palm,
                      all that
Good
    fuss — trust — love — and I
       know not —

Falls away from me now.
Like the two tears from your eyes.
    life and hope had fed, and fed,
    on such,
            and my pace slacknd.

Out the door:
Icy and clear in the dark.
        once I had thought,
        laughing and kissing,
        how cosy to be tuckt in bed —
    let them sleep;
Now I can turn to the hunt.

Blade sharp and hair on end
    over the boulders
    eager
        tasting the snow.

GO ROUND

Plunging donkey   puberty devi
    flings her thighs, swinging long
  legs backward on her mount
hair tosst
        gangle arms but eyes
          her eyes and smile are elsewhere:
swelling out and sailing to the future
  off beyond five-colord clouds.

  we enter this world trailing
        slippery clouds of guts
        incense of our flowery flesh
blossoms; crusht; re-turning
  knots of rose meat open out to — over —
  five-hued clouds —
the empty diamond of all space

And into withered, sturdy, body, stalks.
the dry branch dropping seeds.

       plunging donkey
prancing horse and trappings
  her mother watching,
      shopping bag let down
  beside her knees, against the bench,
in her eyes too the daughter
whirling
looking outward, knowing,

     having once
     steppt up on the
merry-go-
Round.

[*After Rāmprasād Sen*]

Arms shielding my face
Knees drawn up
Falling through flicker
Of womb after womb,
                through worlds,
Only begging, Mother,
                must I be born again?

Snyder says :   you bear me, nurse me
I meet you, always love you,
                you dance
            on my chest and thigh

Forever born again.

IV

THE OLD DUTCH WOMAN

The old dutch woman would spend half a day
Pacing the backyard where I lived
                        in a fixed-up shed,
What did she see.
Wet leaves, the rotten tilted-over
                        over-heavy heads
Of domesticated flowers.
                   I knew Indian Paintbrush
Thought nature meant mountains,
Snowfields, glaciers and cliffs,
White granite waves underfoot.

Heian ladies
Trained to the world of the garden,
                        poetry,
        lovers slippt in with at night —

My Grandmother standing wordless
        fifteen minutes
Between rows of loganberries,
        clippers poised in her hand.

New leaves on the climbing rose
Planted last fall.
    — tiny bugs eating the green —

Like once watching
                   mountaingoats:
Far over a valley
Half into the
                shade of the headwall,
        Pick their way over the snow.

NATURE   GREEN SHIT

The brittle hollow stalks of sunflower
      heads broke over full of dusty seed
      peeld, it tastes good, small

Why should dirt be dirty when you clean up.
      stop to like the dead or dying plants,
      twisted witherd grass

Picking the last peppers
Soft and wrinkld; bright green, cool

      what a lump of red flesh *I* am!

Violet dawn sky — no more Arcturus —
      beside the sugi nursery where we
      pulld down vines
      house lights constellations
      still   on the hill.

Heavy frosted cabbage.
      (all night porch bulb —)
      paper boy squealing bike brakes

      hey that's my cat!
Coming home.

TO THE CHINESE COMRADES

The armies of China and Russia
Stand facing across a wide plain.
Krushchev on one side and Mao on the other,
Krushchev calls out
     "Pay me the money you owe me!"
Mao laughs and laughs. long hair flops.
His face round and smooth.
The armies start marching — they meet —
Without clashing, they march through each other,
Lines between lines.
All the time Mao Tse-tung laughing.
He takes heaps of money.
He laughs and he gives it to Krushchev.

Chairman Mao's belongings on the March :
"Two cotton and wool mixture blankets,
A sheet, two pants and jackets,
A sweater
A patched umbrella
An enamel mug for a rice bowl
A gray brief-case with nine pockets."

Like Han-shan standing there
    — a rubbing off some cliff
Hair sticking out smiling
   maybe rolling a homegrown
   Yenan cigarette
Took a crack at politics
The world is all one.
— crawling out that hillside cave dirt house —

      (whatever happened to Wong —
        quit Chinese school, slugged his dad
        left the laundry, went to sea
        out the golden gate — did he make AB? —)

black eggshell-thin
pots of Lung-shan
maybe three thousand years B C

You have killed
I saw the Tibetans just down from the passes
Limping in high felt boots
Sweating in furs
Flatland heat.

      and from Almora gazing at Trisul
      the new maps from Peking
      call it all China
      clear down to here, & the Gangetic plain —

From Hongkong N.T. on a pine rise
See the other side: stub fields.
Geese, ducks, and children
    far off cries.
Down the river, tiny men
Walk a plank — maybe loading
               little river boat.
Is that China
Flat, brown, and wide?

The ancestors
what did they leave us.
K'ung fu-tze, some buildings, remain.
    — tons of soil gone.
Mountains turn desert.
Stone croppt flood, strippt hills,
The useless wandering river mouths,
Salt swamps
Silt on the floor of the sea.

Wind-borne glacial flour —
Ice-age of Europe,
Dust storms from Ordos to Finland
The loess of Yenan.
    glaciers
         "shrink
and vanish like summer clouds . . ."

CROSS THE SNOWY MOUNTAIN
WE SHALL SEE CHAIRMAN MAO!

The year the long march started I was four.
How long has this gone on.
Rivers to wade, mountains to cross —
Chas. Leong showed me how to hold my chopsticks
                              like the brush —
Upstairs a chinese restaurant catty-corner
                              from the police
Portland, oregon, nineteen fifty-one,
Yakima Indian horseman, hair black as crows.
            shovel shaped incisors,
                epicanthic fold.
Misty peaks and cliffs of the Columbia,
Old loggers vanish in the rocks.
They wouldn't tote me rice and soy-sauce
                              cross the dam
"Snyder you gettin just like
        a damned Chinaman."
Gambling with the Wasco and the Wishram
By the river under Hee Hee Butte
& bought a hard round loaf of weird bread
From a bakery in a tent
In a camp of Tibetans
At Bodh-Gaya
Where Gautama used to stay.

On hearing Joan Baez singing "East Virginia"
        Those were the days.
        we strolld under blossoming cherries
        ten acres of orchard
        holding hands, kissing,
        in the evening talkt Lenin and Marx.
You had just started out for Beijing.

        I slippt my hand under her blouse
        and undid her brassiere.
        I passt my hand over her breasts
        her sweet breath, it was too warm for May.
        I thought how the whole world
        my love, could love like this;
        blossoms, the books, revolution
        more trees, strong girls, clear springs;
You took Beijing

Chairman Mao, you should quit smoking.
>   Dont bother those philosophers
Build dams, plant trees,
>   dont kill flies by hand.
Marx was another westerner.
>   it's all in the head.
You dont need the bomb.
>   stick to farming.
Write some poems. Swim the river.
>   those blue overalls are great.
Dont shoot me, let's go drinking.
>   just
Wait.

FOR THE WEST

1

Europa,
>   your red-haired
>   hazel-eyed
>   Thracian girls
your beautiful thighs
everlasting damnations
and grave insouciance —

a woman's country,
even your fat little popes.
>   groin'd temples
>   groov'd canals
— me too, I see thru
>   these green eyes —

the Cowboys and Indians all over Europe
sliding down snowfields on shields.

what next? a farmer's
corner of the planet —
>   who cares if you are White?

2

this universe — "one turn" — turnd over.
      gods of revolution.
sharp beards — fur flap hats —
                kalmuck whip-swingers,

hugging and kissing
white and black,
men, men,
girls, girls,

wheat, rye, barley,
    adding asses to donkeys
    to fat-haunch horses,
it takes tractors and the
    multiple firing of pistons
to make revolution.
still turning.   flywheel heavy
      elbow-bending awkward
      flippety drive goes
on, white   chicks;

dark skin
      burns the tender lobes.
foggy white skin bleacht out,
pale nipple,
pale breast never freckled,

    they turn and
slowly turn away —

3

    Ah, that's America:
the flowery glistening oil blossom
    spreading on water —
it was so tiny, nothing, now it keeps expanding
all those colors,
              our world
    opening inside outward toward us,
each part swelling and turning
who would have thought such turning;

as it covers,
    the colors fade.
and the fantastic patterns
    fade.
I see down again through clear water.

    it is the same
ball bounce rhyme the
    little girl was singing,
    all those years.

7. IV. 64

up at dawn,
sweep the deck and empty garbage
chip paint down below.
all my friends have children
& I'm getting old. at least enough to be
a First Mate or an Engineer.
now I know I'll never be a Ph.D.
dumping oily buckets
in the middle of the ocean —
swirls of dried
paint drips,
white. silver, blue and green
down the outside,
full of oil — rags —
wet paint slosh coils,
marbled grease and cream.

                pacific near panama

TWELVE HOURS OUT OF NEW YORK AFTER
TWENTY-FIVE DAYS AT SEA

The sun always setting behind us.
I did not mean to come this far.
    — baseball games on the radio
       commercials that turn your hair —
The last time I saild this coast
Was nineteen forty eight
Washing galley dishes
     reading Gide in French.
In the rucksack I've got three *nata*
Handaxes from central Japan;
The square blade found in China
    all the way back to Stone —
A novel by Kafu NAGAI
About geisha in nineteen-ten
With a long thing about gardens
And how they change through the year;
Azalea ought to be blooming
    in the yard in Kyoto now.
Now we are north of Cape Hatteras
Tomorrow docking at eight.
     mop the deck round the steering gear,
Pack your stuff and get paid.

19.IV.1964

ACROSS LAMARCK COL

Descending hillsides in
    half morning light, step over
      small down pine,
I see myself as stony granite face.
All that we did was human,
    stupid, easily forgiven,
Not quite right.

A giving stream you give another
    should have been mine
  had I been not me
      — to whom not given —
Who most needed waited,
Stoppt off, my me, — my fault
    your black block mine — our — ours —
Myself as stony granite face —
You giving him because an   other

I also now become another.
        what I
Had not from you, for you,
      with a new lover,
Give, and give, and give, and
        take.

HOP, SKIP, AND JUMP

for Jim and Annie Hatch

the curvd lines toe-drawn, round cornerd squares
bulge out doubles from its single pillar line, like,
Venus of the Stone Age.
she takes stone,
with a white quartz band for her lagger.
                                        she
    takes a brown-staind salt-sticky cigarette
                        butt.
he takes a mussel shell. he takes a clamshell. she takes
a stick.
he is tiny, with a flying run & leap —
shaggy blond — misses all the laggers,
                tumbles from one foot.
            they are dousing
a girl in a bikini down the beach
                first with cold seawater
                    then with wine.
double-leg   single-leg   stork stalk turn
on the end-square —   hop, fork, hop, scoop the lagger,
        we have all trippt and fallen.
    surf rough and full of kelp,
   all the ages —
draw a line on another stretch of sand —
                        and —
                    everybody try
to do the hop, skip, and jump.

4.X.1964 Muir Beach

AUGUST WAS FOGGY

for Sally

August was foggy,
September dry.
October grew too hot.
Napa and Sonoma grasslands,
          brushlands,
      burned.

In November
      then,
We all set back the clock,
      and suddenly it rained.

The first green shoots of grass.
          you
      like some slender
      fresh young plant
turn smooth and cool across me
      in the night.

touch, and taste, and interlace
      deep in the ground.
          new rain.
as we begin our life.

BENEATH MY HAND AND EYE THE DISTANT HILLS,
YOUR BODY

What my hand follows on your body
Is the line. A stream of love
   of heat, of light,   what my
   eye   lascivious
          licks
   over, watching
   far snow-dappled Uintah mountains
Is that stream.
Of power.   what my
   hand curves over, following the line.
      "hip" and "groin"

Where "I"
   follow by hand and eye
   the swimming limit of your body.
As when vision idly dallies on the hills
Loving what it feeds on.
   soft cinder cones and craters;
     — Drum Hadley in the Pinacate
       took ten minutes more to look again —
A leap of power unfurling:
    left,   right — right —
My heart beat faster looking
   at the snowy Uintah mountains.

As my hand feeds on you
   runs down your side and curls beneath your hip.
   oil pool; stratum; water —

What "is" within   not known
   but feel it
   sinking with a breath
   pusht ruthless, surely, down.

Beneath this long caress of hand and eye
   "we" learn the flower burning,
      outward, from "below".

THE PLUM BLOSSOM POEM

Angel island.
The sailboat slipping barely west,
Floating over coiling
        tongues of filling mud.
East face of the Sierra still is
      tilting;
Two plums below Buchanan street
     on Vallejo
Blow blossom petals
      eastward down the walk.
We hold and caress each other
Where a world is yet unborn;
Long slow swells in the Pacific —
      the land drifts north.

THROUGH THE SMOKE HOLE

for Don Allen

I

There is another world above this one; or outside of this one; the way to it is thru the smoke of this one, & the hole that smoke goes through. The ladder is the way through the smoke hole; the ladder holds up, some say, the world above; it might have been a tree or pole; I think it is merely a way.

Fire is at the foot of the ladder. The fire is in the center. The walls are round. There is also another world below or inside this one. The way there is down thru smoke. It is not necessary to think of a series.

Raven and Magpie do not need the ladder. They fly thru the smoke holes shrieking and stealing. Coyote falls thru; we recognize him only as a clumsy relative, a father in old clothes we don't wish to see with our friends.

It is possible to cultivate the fields of our own world without much thought for the others. When men emerge from below we see them as the masked dancers of our magic dreams. When men disappear down, we see them as plain men going somewhere else. When men disappear up we see them as great heroes shining through the smoke. When men come back from above they fall thru and tumble; we don't really know them; Coyote, as mentioned before.

II

Out of the kiva come
masked dancers or
plain men.
        plain men go into the ground.

out there out side all the chores
        wood and water, dirt,
wind, the view across the flat,
here, in the round
                        no corners
head is full of magic figures —

woman your secrets aren't my secrets
what I cant say I wont
walk round
put my hand flat down.
you in the round too.
gourd vine blossom.
walls and houses drawn up
from the same soft soil.

thirty million years gone
        drifting sand.
  cool rooms pink stone
worn down fort floor, slat sighting
   heat shine on jumna river

dry wash, truck tracks in the riverbed
coild sand pinyon.

      seabottom
      riverbank
      sand dunes
the floor of a sea once again.

      human fertilizer
      underground water tunnels
      skinny dirt gods
      grandmother berries
              out
through the smoke hole.
   (for childhood and youth *are* vanity

a Permian reef of algae,

out through the smoke hole
swallowd sand
       salt mud
swum bodies,   flap
to the limestone blanket —

lizzard tongue,   lizzard tongue

   wha, wha, wha flying
in and *out* thru the smoke hole

      plain men
   come out of the ground.

OYSTERS

First   Samish Bay.
      then all morning, hunting oysters

A huge feed on white
wood State Park slab-plank bench-
                    and table
                        at Birch Bay
                    where we picked up rocks
      for presents.

And ate oysters, fried — raw — cookt in milk
      rolld in crumbs —
all we wanted.

               ALL WE WANTED

& got back in our wagon,
drove away.

V

Miyazawa Kenji

MIYAZAWA Kenji (1896-1933)

. . . was born and lived most his life in Iwate prefecture in northern Japan. This area, sometimes called the Tibet of Japan, is known for poverty, cold, and heavy winter snows. His poems are all from there.

He was born and lived his life among the farmers: a school-teacher (Chemistry, Natural Sciences, Agriculture) and a Buddhist. His poems have many Buddhist allusions, as well as scientific vocabulary.

The bulk of his work is colloquial and metrically free. His complete work, published after his death, contains seven hundred free-verse poems, nine hundred *tanka* poems, and ninety children's stories.

REFRACTIVE INDEX

This one of the seven forests:
more light than under water —
and vast.
tramping up a frozen rutted road,
rutted snow,
toward those shrivelled zinc clouds —
like a melancholick mailman
      (or Aladdin with his lamp —)
must I hurry so?

THE SNOW ON SADDLE MOUNTAIN

The only thing that can be relied on
is the snow on Kurakake Mountain.
fields and woods
thawing, freezing, and thawing,
totally untrustworthy.
it's true, a great fuzzy windstorm
like yeast up there today, still
the only faint source of hope
is the snow on Kurakake mountain.

SPRING AND THE ASHURA

From the ash-colored steel of images:
akebia tendrils coil round clouds,
wildrose thicket, swampy leafmold —
everywhere a pattern of flattery
    (amber splinters flooding down
      thicker than woodwinds at noon)
the bitter taste of anger, the blueness.
at the depths in the brilliance of this april air
spitting, gnashing, pacing back and forth
I am an Ashura!
    (the scene gets blurred by tears)
smashed bits of cloud cross my vision,
    a holy crystal wind sweeps
      the translucent sea of the sky.
        Zypressen — one line of spring
        blackly draws in ether,
          — through those dark footsteps
            the edge of the mountain of heaven shines.
        (shimmering mist, white polarization)
      the true words are lost.
     turn, clouds flying
   ah, in the radiant depths of april
  gnashing, BURNING, wander
I am one of the Ashuras:
  (chalcedony clouds flowing
    where is that singing, that spring bird?)
  Sun Wheel shimmering blue
    ashura echoing in the forest
      heaven's bowl giddily tilting over
        clusters of giant coal-fern stretch up toward it.
        pitifully dense — those branches
    this whole double scene.
   flash of a crow flapping
             up from a treetop
      — spiritless woods —
      — the atmosphere clearer and clearer
        cypress trees standing to heaven
           in a dead hush —
a thing in the golden meadow:
just a person.
farmer wearing a straw cape looking at me
can he really see me
at the bottom of this shining sea of air?

blue over blue, deepening my sadness.
zypressen silently quivering
    bird again cuts the blue
        (my real feelings are not here
        ashura tears on the ground)

breathing anew   in the sky
lungs faintly contracting
    (this body totally dispersed
      mixed with the atoms of space)

twigs of a gingko still reflecting
cypress blacker and blacker
sparks of cloud pour down.

NOTE

Ashura is a Sanskrit Buddhist term for beings inhabiting one of the six realms of existence. They are malevolent giants in constant strife, often represented in art as human warriors, samurai, killing each other. The ashura realm is the warring, contentious, hostile area of the mind. The other five realms are hell-dwellers, hungry ghosts, animals, mankind, and devas.

CLOUD SEMAPHORE

Ah, it's great! clear — clean —
wind blowing
farm tools twinkling
vague mountains
   — lava-plug   magma
all in a dream where there's no time

     when cloud semaphores
     were already hung
     in the stark blue east

the vague mountains . . .
    wild geese will come
       down to the four
          cedars tonight!

THE SCENE

Clouds volatile as carbonic acid
blossoming cherries glow in the sun
wind comes again over the grasses
clipped tara trees tremble

    — just finished spreading manure
            in the sandy loam
      now it's all a picture in cobalt glaze.

heedless larks dumdum bullets
suddenly shoot out of the sky —

wind wipes away this blue stupor
gold grass quivering

clouds volatile as carbonic acid
cherry shines white in the sun.

A BREAK

Up in that gaudy space's
upper section a buttercup is blooming
      (high-class buttercup it is but
        rather than butter, from sulphur and honey)
below that, wild parsley and clover
and a dragonfly of worked tinplate.
rain crackles,
    oriole cries in the
      silverberry tree ...
stretch out on the grass,
there's white and black both in the clouds;
it all goes shining, seething up.
fling off my hat it's the sooty cap of a mushroom
roll over and tilt my head back
           over the edge of the dike.
yawn; shiny demons come out of space.
   this hay's soft, it's a first-rate bed.

clouds all picked to bits,
the blue becomes eyes in a huge net, an
underlying glimmering steel plate

          oriole without break —
        sunshining   crackling

DAWN

Rolling snow turned peach-color
        the moon
      left alone in the fading night
makes a soft cry in the heavens
and once more
drinks up the scattered light

(*parasamgate, bodhi, svaha !*)

119

SOME VIEWS CONCERNING THE PROPOSED SITE
OF A NATIONAL PARK

Well how do you like this lava flow?
not very scenic, is it.
don't know how long ago it was spit out
on a sunny day like this you see the heat waves
just like a huge pan
and the snow up on the peak blue and simmering
say, have a sandwich.
why on earth don't you want to
develop this area?
it's a real good possibility —
mountains all around
crater lakes, hot springs, right there.
Saddle Mountain
well of course Saddle Mountain
and that big crater's probably
older than hell itself.
why sure! you could fix it up like Hell
with a real oriental charm to it, huh
a stockade of red spears
weird-shaped old dead trees put around
and plant flowers here and there,
well, flowers, I mean sort of things like uh
jimsonweed and viper grass
black wolfsbane and such
anyhow, make it gruesome, huh.
tourists will flock from all over.
we could get some mean looking guys
shave their heads
and make gates out of rock here and there
and drag the folks that come, around barefoot
            — you know —
by the "cuckoo singing on the path after death"
and the "ford of the river of the three ways"
"the gate to the new womb" at Yama's office
then, having expiated all their sins
we can sell them certificates for Heaven.
afterwards — at those three wooded hills
we could put on symphonies, huh
first movement: allegro con brio, like springing forth
second movement: sort of "andante"

third movement: like a lament
fourth movement: feeling of death
you know how it goes — at first kind of sorrowful
then bit by bit getting joyous.
at the end, on this side of the hill
hide two field-cannons
shoot them off — live shells — with a bang, by electricity.
just when they're feeling A-1
they'll *really* think they're on the
                    River of the Three Ways, huh
us we'll have had lots of practice
we won't be scared at all
I wouldn't be a bit flustered
say, have one of those sandwiches
that hill over there — really drizzling, eh?
like a picture in blue on a porcelain
that fellow will make a good backdrop, huh.

COW

An ayrshire cow
playing, rubbing her horns in the grass,
                    in the misty soil,
at her back the pulp factory fires
scorch the night clouds.
over low dunes
the sea booms
            a brass moon
like you could scoop up and swallow

so the cow feels pretty good
playing now
tapping the fence with her horns.

FLOATING WORLD PICTURE:
SPRING IN THE KITAGAMI MOUNTAINS

1

Nobody at the edge of the firepit
snowboots and jute leggings.
white birch flaming
jetting out sour hot sap
— a child sings the kite song
skinning badgers.
housepillars gleaming with soot
    — like shaped with stone axes —
the sheer ceiling
full of the blue smoke of breakfast
— vault of a temple —
one shaft of sunlight shooting down and
        all is at the bottom in that
                sensual beam of light.

Spring — at the chilly horsebarn
glimmer of dry hay and snow
yearning for sunny hills
the horses stamp their hooves.

2

The willow puts out honey flowers
birds flow over hill after hill
horses hurry:
        hot-breatht Arab
        glistening light-bodied thoroughbred
invisible cuneiform wind
in the stiff gloomy limbs of the walnut —
a dog rustles in bamboo grass.

        heavy work horse
        flashing his tufty tail
        like a monstrous lizard
                navigating in the sun

horses one by one coming,
chewing at the edge of the marl,
climbing along the misty run of snowmelt
under a malachite sky
— bright noisy market --
being led to the
stud inspection center.

ORDERS

The minus-1 Infantry Company
Leaves bivouac at 1 AM
From the present row of pine advancing
          in a southerly direction
Over there,
That
There uh
That black tree standing alone, proceed
To set your course by the green star visible
          two fingers to the right of the top
          of it
Toward the headwaters,
And attack and destroy the glow of the
          lights from the town.
Leader of Platoon number 1
You can swallow down your great sleepiness
While marching.
Now at the environs of the municipality
In the swamp running along the edge of the
          roadside trees
Waterlily and Junsai
And swampfire flickering on and off.
No need to bother about that.
Very well. You all understand?
End of orders.

DISTANT LABOR

Beyond the pampas-grass flowers
        and the dark grove
a new sort of wind is blowing
— through dazzling wrinkly cloud fretwork
                and spring sun
with a shiver of strange odors.

And from the hill behind the empty creek
and the barely rising black smoke
of the tileworks
a big cheerful racket.

— listening in the farmers fields
it seems pleasant enough work all right
but every night Chuichi
comes home from there exhausted
                and bad-tempered.

THE POLITICIANS

Running around here & there
stirring up trouble and bothering people
a bunch of lushes —
        fern leaves and cloud:
the world was so chilly and dark —

Before long that sort
will up and rot all by themselves
and be washed away by the rain
and afterwards, only green fern.

And when humanity is laid out like coal
somewhere some earnest geologist
will note them in his notebook.

MOON, SON OF HEAVEN

When I was a child
in all sorts of magazines and newspapers
   — how many — photographs of the moon;
face scarred by jagged craters.
I clearly saw that the sun light strikes it.
later I learned it's terribly cold
           and no air.
maybe three times I saw it eclipsed —
the earth's shadow
slipped over it, clearly.
next, that it probably broke off from earth.
and last, a fellow I met during rice planting
    from the Morioka meteorological observatory
    once showed me that heavenly body through
    a something-mm little telescope
    and explained how its orbit and motions
accord with a simple formula.

However. ah,
for me in the end there's no obstacle
to reverently titling that heavenly body
Emperor Moon.
if someone says
   man is his body
   that's a mistake.
   and if someone says
   man is body and mind
   that too is an error
   and if one says man is mind,
   still it's wrong.

so — I —
hail the moon as Emperor Moon.
this is not mere personification.

DAYDREAMING ON THE TRAIL

A lonely stretch, in the bind of poor fishing
                              & drouth,
following the ocean
crossing pass after pass,
fields of wild reeds,
I've come this far alone.

dozing in the pale sun
on the sand of a dried-up riverbed
back and shoulder chilled
something bothering me —
I think at that last quartzite pass
I left the oak gate in the fence
of the cowpasture open
probably because I was hurrying —
                    a white gate —
did I close it or not?

light cool sky,
mistletoe on chestnut floats in vision
manylayered clouds upriver
cool lattice of sunlight
some unknown big bird   calling
faintly, crork   crork

THE GREAT POWER LINE POLE

rain and clouds drift to the ground
susuki-grass red ears washed
fields fresh and live
and the great power line pole of Hanamaki
sparrows on a hundred insulators
then off to pillage a ricefield
whish whish whish whish flying
light of rain and cloud
and nimbly sweeping back to the hundred insulators
at the fork in the Hanamaki road
sparrows

PINE NEEDLES

    some raindrops still clinging
— I brought you these pine boughs

— you look like you'd jump up
& put your hot cheek against this green,
fiercely thrust your cheek
into the blue pine needles
greedily
— you're going to startle the others —
did you want to go to the woods
                         that much?
burning with fever
tormented by sweat and pain

And me working happily in the sunlight
Thinking of you, walking slowly through the trees
      "Oh I'm all right now
        it's like you brought the
        center of the forest right here. . ."

Like a bird or a squirrel
you long for the woods.
how you must envy me,
my sister, who this very day must
      travel terribly far.
can you manage it alone?
      ask me to go with you
        crying — ask me —
your cheeks however
how beautiful they are.

I'll put these fresh pine boughs
on top of the mosquito net
they may drip a little
ah, a clean
smell like turpentine.

THIEF

About when the stars of the Skeleton
      were paling in the dawn:
Striding the crackly glitter
      — frozen mud —
The thief who had just stolen a celadon vase
      from the front of a store
Suddenly stopped those long black legs
Covered his ears with his hands
And listened to the humming of his mind.